PRAYERS
FOR
ATHLETES

By Rena Boston

True Victory is in GodTrust Him to lead you

REMEMBER:

Victory Does not Always mean You win!

Rather, It means You gave it Your best!

ISBN 978-0-9972297-0-7

For licensing/copyright information, for additional copies, or for
use in specialized settings, contact:

Just Writers Publishing Company
Where Fingers Write From The Heart
Round Lake, Illinois 60073
(847) 494-8420 (direct)
www.justwriters.com
renaboston@comcast.net
justwriters@comcast.net

TABLE OF CONTENTS

DEDICATION

This book is dedicated to my daughter, LeTrisha Daniel, who placed her life on hold to prepare her three sons, Kenneth Jr., Kristopher, and Kaleb for life. This included their spiritual and natural lives. What she has imparted into her sons is enough to take them through life; however, she never stopped at enough. She continues to instill in them, excellence.

No sacrifice was too great. Sleepless nights and hardship did not deter her. Despite becoming a single parent when her sons were ages 6, 8 and 9, her dreams for them remained alive. Dreams that only a mother, who singlehandedly homeschooled and nurtured them for over 15 years, could envision.

LeTrisha and her husband happily dwelled together during the early years of the boys life. This made my heart glad. I rejoiced because I believed my grandsons would receive something neither LeTrisha nor I had received, a good father image. Her husband was a good father until he turned his back on the family and walked away to another life when the boys were ages 6, 8, and 9.

Regardless of being deserted, she was determined to follow the paths God had opened for her sons. Im sure she would love to have had someone by her side to encourage her, to tell her she was doing a great job. Nevertheless, she was motivated by a single command from God. Hed told her to leave Corporate America and Go home and nurture your sons.

These boys are a part of my Legacy, so I felt compelled to leave on record, a small contribution to the foundation that LeTrisha has already established. I encourage Kenneth Jr., Kristopher and Kaleb to regularly pray these prayers.

This book is also dedicated to my daughter, Jeanine Joe, and granddaughter, Ashley. Jeanine is also a single parent and has been a single parent since Ashleys birth. She has dedicated her life ensuring that her daughter is thoroughly equipped to fulfill her dreams. Over a span of years, Jeanine simultaneously worked fulltime, attended college fulltime, and singlehandedly provided parental guidance for Ashley. She has sacrificed her dreams and delayed finishing college for her masters to ensure that Ashley receives the development she will need in life. When Ashley was very young, Jeanine placed a violin in her hands, and she is now a member of the Milwaukee Symphony.

Sports are a secondary aspiration for Ashley. Her goal is to become a doctor. I encourage her to fulfill her dreams. I also encourage her to pray the prayers in this handbook. These prayers will strengthen and sustain her. Whether in sports or not, this book is for Ashley also, the other portion of my Legacy.

This book is also dedicated to (mom) Mother Mary A. Moody. We have not received a greater display of love, prayer, and support than that from mom. She has counseled, instructed, and encouraged all of us many times. There are not adequate words to describe the pillar of strength she has been for us. Mom has always been accessible when we needed her. We appreciate you so very much, mom.

This book is dedicated to Athletes everywhere. Any Athlete willing to talk with God is encouraged to own a copy of this book.

With love,
GG

THE GRANDS, MY HEARTBEAT

A RELEASE INTO YOUR SPIRITS

Kenneth Jr.,
Kristopher,
Kaleb,

Within each of you resides:
* wisdom like Solomon,
* strength like Samson,
* worship like David, and,
* anointing like Paul;

so let them come forth in all you say and do!

Ashley,

Within you reside:
* wisdom like Abigail,
* love like Esther,
* leadership like Deborah, and,
* anointing like Mary;

so let them come forth in all you say and do!

With love,
GG

APPRECIATION

I am deeply touched and appreciative for all Bishop Carlis L. Moody, Sr., James Ranger, Coach DeShawn Curtis, Coach Darryl Brooks, Sr., and Coach Jason Price, imparted into the lives of my grandsons. Your sacrifices have not gone unnoticed.

Thank you dad (Bishop Moody) for being strength to my three generations. You have been a dad to me, a granddad to my daughters, and a great-granddad to my grandchildren. And we say, Thank You. Thank you for all of your sacrifices. All we received from you personally and across the pulpit have created a firm foundation for life. We have built upon that foundation and have not been ashamed.

Thank you Big Guy (James) for being a Christian role model for my grandchildren. Thank you for sharing the true principles of life with them. Thank you for being a strong male figure for them to respect and emulate. Thank you for the special bond you share with them.

Thank you DeShawn for seeing the potential in my grandsons and doing all you did to bring it forth. Thank you for being stern with them. Thank you for driving and pushing them to excellence. We can never pay you for your sacrifices or the level of influence youve had in the development of their skills in sport. Thank you for being A Friend to LeTrisha.

Thank you Coach Brooks and Coach Price for your encouragement and trust in my grandsons sports abilities. Both of you were buffers for them. You provided them with a level of comfort, which enabled them to trust their gifts. Words dont seem sufficient, but I thank you from the bottom of my heart!

With love,
GG

FOREWORD

As a Sports Fan, I cringe when I see a player suffering an injury. My first instinct is to utter a prayer for their healing and recovery.

I believe this book is very timely and on target, encouraging prayer before entering the sports arena, regardless the sport. Watching my grandchildren actively engaging in various sports gives me a special appreciation for this book.

The players can pray for themselves and each other. They can pray with the confidence of knowing that God hears and answers prayers. The prayers are basic, yet, specific. Every Team within each sport can pray the prayer, which directly addresses what they are facing.

I encourage you to pray, believe, and receive answers to your prayers.

James Ranger, President/CEO
Ranger Remodeling Services
Husband
Father
Grandfather

INTRODUCTION

This book is written to promote prayer in the lives of my athletic grandsons, Kenneth Daniel Jr., Kristopher Daniel, and Kaleb Daniel, my gifted granddaughter, Ashley Joe-Fuqua, **and any athlete willing to talk with God.**

You are encouraged to pray a prayer before engaging in any activity. Start your day with a conversation with God. He will speak and you can respond. You can speak and He will respond. Rest your head upon His shoulder. Prayer relaxes you.

We must always pray, so we wont faint. Prayer is to the spirit, what breath is to the body, LIFE!

As you pray these prayers, you are encouraged to add your own heart and spirit to them. They are LIFE to those who pray them.

LET
US
PRAY

LIFE

Father God, your Word gives light and cleanses
our hearts. Your Word has increased our
understanding of life, and has made us wiser than
our enemies. We have been taught what is good
and what is right. Give us this day, success
we pray.
Amen!

HEALTH

Father God, we thank you for our mental, physical and spiritual health. Our wellbeing is in its fullness. Our friendships and other relationships are blessed. You have anointed those around us and removed those who were against us. Our hearts are in unity. Our unity will increase our strength, and our strength will lead us to victory, we pray.

Amen!

Opportunity

Father God, we thank you for opening doors of opportunity for us. Thank you for giving us the wisdom to take advantage of every opportunity. We pray for the strength and courage to move forward. We pray that victory and success are manifested this day in our lives.

Amen!

GODS CONTROL

Father God, take control of every area of our lives. Everywhere we go let your presence go with us. Make us sensitive to your voice. Be with us as we go to conquer and dominate, in the task that is before us. Thank you for extending your mercy to us. Amen!

PROTECTION

Father God, we thank you for being our protection. Your eyes see everything. You see the good and the evil. You protect us and guard us against evil intentions. You protect our reputation, our name, and our character. Thank you for watching over us and maintaining our lives. Victory is ours, we pray. Amen!

DIRECTION

Father God, we ask you to direct our footsteps today. We will go where you lead us. Give us dominion over our opponents. Let all we do today be acceptable in your sight. You are our dwelling place and our shield of protection.

Thank you for the victory.

Amen!

EXPECTATIONS

Father God, we thank you for giving us hope when doubt and fear enter our hearts. We move forward with great expectations. We are excited for what you will do through us. We release your power and authority into our lives. We walk in conquering power. We are bold and strong in you.

We are victorious.

Amen!

LEADERS

Father God, we stand in the gap for our Coaches. We ask you to give them mercy and grace. Reward them for the sacrifices they have made. They have trained and helped us develop the skills we needed to succeed. Let us go forth and fully demonstrate what they have imparted into our lives. Let us be a beacon of light for them to see their work and labor of love, we pray.

Amen!

EMOTIONS

Father God, you alone know our hearts. Search our hearts and remove whatever is not pleasing to you. Dont allow anger and contention to separate us. We will not give place to jealousy. We will unite as one and move forward to accomplish our task at hand.

Amen!

HOPE

Father God, our hope is in you. Without you, we can do nothing. Uphold us today and let us not be ashamed. Hold us up as we glorify your name in all we do. We can do great things when you are at the helm of our lives. Thank you for a day of victory, we pray.

Amen!

DESTINY

Father God, you said your thoughts about us are peaceful thoughts, to give us an expected end. Dont let us lose our focus. Help us to keep our eyes on the prize. Enlighten our hearts to reach our destiny. Today we will pursue it, and we ask you to deliver victory into our hands.

We will give you the glory.

Amen!

DISTRACTIONS

Father God, we bring you all of our distractions.
Our attention cannot be divided while we seek
to accomplish our task. We cast all of our cares
upon you. We give you the concerns of our heart.
Restore wholeness to us, so we can fulfill
our mission, we pray.
Amen!

OPEN HANDS

Father God, be with us. You open your hand
and satisfy the desire of every living thing. Open
your hand to us today and satisfy the desires of
our hearts. You are true and faithful. You always
fulfill your promises to your people. Watch over
us and produce fruit in our lives that will
glorify you.

Amen!

EMPOWERMENT

Father God, we humbly come to you. We are the work of your hands. We can do nothing without you. Empower us with your power that all will see your glory, as we go forth today. Protect us and keep all hurt, harm, and danger from us.

Amen!

MIRACLE

Father God, we worship and honor the miracle working power in your Word. We ask you to work a miracle for us today. Remove all doubt and questions from our hearts. Let us rest in you, who will cause us to triumph this day.

Amen!

ENERGY

Thank you Father God for this day. When our bodies get tired, refresh us and revive our spirits.

Energize us beyond our imagination.

We will abide under your shadow. Give rest to our weary bodies and strengthen those who have no strength, we pray.

Amen!

HIS PRESENCE

Father God, we know you are with us. Your presence has sustained us. You are our solid foundation. You do for us that which no man can do. We thank you for being with us. Bless us this day, we pray.

Amen!

FAVOR

Father God, we are blessed because of your favor. You have covered us. You have kept us from stumbling. We have refrained from evil and wrong doings. We are focused, and our hearts and eyes are turned away from vanity. Lead us this day into your victory.

Amen!

PLOTS

Father God, we speak your power over our life.
We cancel every plot, plan, scheme, and strategy
that the enemy has devised against us. No weapon
formed against us will prosper. We are more than
conquerors today. We ask you to show
forth your power.
Amen!

THE CENTER

Thank you Father, for your divine favor to us.
We are blessed and highly favored. Thank you
for being the center of our lives. You give life to
every dead situation involving us. Thank you for
your resurrection power, in every situation
we might face.

Amen!

LOVE

Father God, you are love. Help us to represent you with love. Let others look at us and see you in our lives and actions. Let the life we live show forth your character. Dont let bad attitudes darken your light in our lives. Bless us to go forth and conquer.

Amen!

CHALLENGES

Father God, we stand before you totally transparent. You told us to come and bring the conditions of our hearts to you. Here we are before your throne seeking help. You promised that your arms and ears were open to us. You see our challenges. We need you in every area of our lives. Help us to succeed we pray.

Amen!

UNITY

Father God, unite us as a Team. Being united will make us strong. Trust will raise us up above our opponents. We give you the walls, which we have built up. Help us tear them down, remove them, and run to win.

Amen!

VENGEANCE

Father God, forgive us of our sins. We will
not overly concern ourselves with Teams who
practice doing wrong. Vengeance belongs to you.
You will repay. We will all reap what we sow.
Keep us free from the power of revenge. Let our
light shine today, as we defeat our opponents.

Amen!

PERSEVERANCE

Father God, you have raised us up, high above our circumstances. There is nothing too hard for us to accomplish when we trust you. Thank you in advance for the victory. We will run and not get weary. We will pursue to the end.

Amen!

LEAD

Father God, teach us the good way, wherein we should walk. Give us light in darkness. When we cant see our way, let your mercy and grace rest upon us. Lead us in the path of victory. We will follow where you lead, because we know you are with us.

Amen!

PEACE

Father God, we know you are the Prince of Peace. We declare today, we will abide in your peace. Things around us will not trouble us. All of our concerns and fears are wiped away by your peace. We are confident that we will be victorious, because you are on our side. Amen!

FOCUS

Father God, we thank you for the favor you have given us. We dwell in safety with you. Please keep our hearts and minds focused. We surrender our ways to you, and we receive your divine intervention.

We will not stray from the things we were taught.

Amen!

EXAMPLES

Father God, let the life we live be clean.
Strengthen us to think, speak, and do the right
things. Let us be examples that others can follow.
When others look at us, let them see the hope
and trust we have in you. Be with us as we move
forward today.
Amen!

COMMITTED

Father God, let your light shine in the corners of our hearts. Cause us to examine ourselves and see if we are totally committed to the task before us. Give us the endurance we need to succeed.

Amen!

REMEMBER

Father God, stir up our hearts and minds. Cause us to remember all of the previous victories you have given us. We bow our hearts to you in gratitude. Thank you for your goodness. Equip us to go forth in your wisdom and strength. Enable us to accomplish what we have been chosen to accomplish.

Amen!

LIGHT

Father God, we honor your Word. It is a lamp unto our feet, and a light unto our path. As we fulfill this task today, show us how to move wisely and skillfully. Thank you that our advocate stands in the gap for us. As we move forward, we will not be distracted. We refuse to walk in fear, because we have the victory.

Amen!

GUIDANCE

Father God, we thank you for establishing our Team, as a tower and a fortress. In you, we have the victory. We are empowered to succeed. We are committed to your guidance, and the teachings we have received.

Thank you for this victory.

Amen!

SKILLS

Father God, we place our lives in your hand.
Shield and protect us as we fulfill this task
today. You knew us before we were born, and
you placed within each of us, all that is needed to
be victorious today. We will go forward knowing,
we live, move and have our abilities in you.

Amen!

PURPOSE

Father God, we ask that you would prepare us to fulfill your purpose for our lives. We will go where you send us, speak what you command, and do what is right. As we face each challenge, let us be a reflection of you.

Give us the victory, we pray.

Amen!

OPEN DOORS

Father God, we thank you for giving us your
strength when we are weak. You have opened
doors for us in many arenas. Our help comes
from you, the Creator of heaven and earth. You
have maintained our footsteps. All that we have
accomplished was by your spirit.

Help us again today, we pray.

Amen!

HIS PRESENCE

Father God, your presence holds us steady and keeps us level headed. You refresh us when we are faint, and encourage us to continue until the end. We walk in your truth and are sealed. Thank you for giving us the victory today. Amen!

AVAILABLE

Father God, we belong to you. Use us like you used Jehoshaphat. When all the odds were against him, you won the victory for him and he didnt even have to fight. As we go out to slay our giants, go with us. We thank you for using us. Despite what comes our way, we will trust you to lead us to victory.

Amen!

Strategies

Father God, you developed ways and strategies for us, in our most difficult times, which brought us victories. You led us in a clear path. As we went step-by-step, you opened the way before us. Thank you for directing our footsteps. We honor you for who you are.

Amen!

Our Cares

Father God, we cast all of our cares upon you. We know you care about us. We cast our actions, reactions, and attitudes upon you. Despite our faults and failures, we will never let go of your hand. You are the reason that we press forward, towards the mark of excellence. Thank you for our achievements today.

Amen!

VESSELS OF HONOR

Father God, you have made us a light in the
world. Let our light shine that others might
glorify your name. We submit our will to you.
You are the Creator and we are the clay. Make us
and mold us into the vessel you have called us to
be. Equip us for the task today we pray.
Amen!

CONQUERORS

Father God, we are more than conquerors through Christ who loves us. We have been made overcomers by his shed blood. We are the resources he uses to accomplish his will in the earth. We work with the plan you designed for our lives. We are victorious through Christ.

Amen!

THE PLAN

Father God, we come to you in the power of your Word. We are complete in you. Your Word is the head of all principalities and powers. It has sustained us. You have brought us into the fullness of the plan for our lives. Thank you for equipping us to fulfill our purposes in life.

Amen!

COMPLETENESS

Father God, we thank you for our completeness. In you, we are whole and lack nothing. We can achieve whatsoever task that is assigned to us. We are kept in safety wherever we go. You have given your angels charge over us, to protect us. Thank you for blessing our going out and our coming in. Amen!

PREPARATION

Father God, you have prepared us for the task that is before us. You have anointed our heads with oil. Our ability to achieve our goals is overflowing. Your goodness and mercy are with us, to help us fulfill our calling. Thank you. Amen!

Surrender

Father God, we surrender our ways and actions to you today. You are just and righteous. We trust you with all of our heart. We know you will bring us to the expected end you have planned for us. You have designed our paths, and we will walk therein. We pray for victory.

Amen!

PATIENCE

Father God, we patiently wait for you. We believe you see us, you know about us, and you care for us. You are in control of our lives. You hold the reigns to our hearts and direct our course. If you dont lead us to victory, we wont succeed. We are in your care. Go with us, we pray.

Amen!

IDENTITY

Father God, as we go forward today, we ask you to place your arms around us, and protect us from danger, seen and unseen. Keep all hurt and harm away from us. We belong to you. We are identified with you. We are known by your name. We have been observed bowing to you for guidance. Thank you for our shield of protection. Amen!

DREAMS

Father God, we thank you for blessing our going out and our coming in. Thank you for enabling us to realize our dreams and visions. Let your blessings overtake us today. Bless and multiply the work of our hands. Be glorified as we go forth in your name.

Amen!

CHOSEN

Father God, we are available vessels for you to use. Our lives reveal your glory. We can do nothing without you. We are your servants and we walk in your grace. We are chosen and anointed to fulfill your call in our lives. We are victorious in all things. Be glorified we pray. Amen!

BLESSED

Father God, we belong to you. And as your children, we decree that everything our hands do is abundantly blessed. Our mouths are filled with good things. We respect authority and obey the laws. We are filled with the love of God. We walk upon our high places. We trample on defeat. You sustain us in all our endeavors. Thank you.

Amen!

SUCCESS

Father God, we proclaim eternal victory in our lives. Let your divine wisdom and heavenly strategies sustain us. We pray all remains well as we obey the instructions given to us. Father, dont let us forget that you are the center and success of all our efforts.

We cannot make it without you.

Amen!

DIVISION

Father God, shake us and stir us up! Cause us to
remember that a divided team cannot progress.
Let peace reign, knowing that each of us was
designed to accomplish a specific task. Let us
respect one another and the task assigned to each
of us. Dont allow us to devour each other with
our words, we pray.

Amen!

COMPETITION

Father God, open our eyes to see clearly, we are on the same team. We are not here to compete with each other. We are here, to work together as one, a team. We will operate in sync with each other to the degree our actions are seamless. Let every action taken, be a compliment to each other we pray.

Amen!

HUMILITY

Father God, free us from ourselves. Dont let
us think more of ourselves than we should. Let
us walk in humility. We will not listen to, or say
things to put others down. We will not insult
other teammates. We will not use sharp, harsh or
profane words. Despite bad behavior from other
teams, we will not retaliate. We bring our temper
under control. We will respect others
and ourselves.
Amen!

JUSTICE

Father God, we come against bad sportsmanship. We bind every evil strategy, plot, and plan the other teams may have. We pray our work is judged in fairness and equity. You control the hearts of those in authority. Redirect and purify evil hearts. Elevate the pure hearts. Let justice prevail we pray.

Amen!

WARRIOR

Father God, we come to obtain mercy and find grace to help in our time of need. We believe you can and will deliver us. We ask you to abide with us. Take control of every situation that arises today. Give us the spirit of a warrior, like David. Let us go forth and come back as the head, because you are with us.

Amen!

CHAMPIONS

Father God, we believe there is a champion inside of us. Help us to be bold and strong as a lion. We will do what we need to do, and then watch you deliver our opponents into our hands. Give us a hunger and a thirst for this championship. We will diligently pursue it. Bless us with courage.

Amen!

HIGH PLACES

Father God, in your authority we will walk upon our high places this day. We will take back what the enemy stole from us. Let life-giving words flow from our mouths. Reveal yourself in our midst. You are the solution to all of our problems and the answer to all of our questions. We are looking to you for help, guidance, and deliverance.

Amen!

ONENESS

Father God, we pray you would bring us together as one. Let us listen to one another, and be slow to speak. Let us not judge one another, but encourage and build one another up. Help us to keep our tongues from speaking negative things. We will fortify ourselves by thinking the best about each other.

Amen!

CIRCUMSTANCES

Father God, remember us in our circumstances. You are our shepherd and we lack nothing. Our hope and trust are in you. Our eyes are upon you. We will look to you for all we need. We depend on you. You are our sustainer.

You are our life.

Amen!

Open Arms

Father God, we thank you for access into your presence. You have opened your arms and welcomed us. Your eyes have watched over us. Your ears are open to our cry. When our backs were against the wall, you picked us up and comforted us. Thank you for not withdrawing your hands from us. We need you. Stay with us. Amen!

PRIDE

Father God, you are our life and the length of our days. We are nothing without you. We are only complete when we dwell in you.

Let us not be lofty and lifted up, because pride can destroy us. Let us be examples of you, among the heathen. Go with us and stand by us continuously. Thank you for the victory.

Amen!

FUTURE

Father God, we pray for our future. We dwell with a mixed multitude of people, where right seems wrong and wrong seems right. We dwell where evil is getting more and more rampant. Dont allow sin to pollute our hearts. Cover us and let others see you in our lives.

Amen!

VULNERABLE

Father God, we decree we shall not be
vulnerable. Our eyes are open and we will not
fall into darkness. Thank you for keeping our
hearts and minds clean. You have kept us from
lying down in shame, and rising up in disgrace.
We thank you that we are like trees planted by
rivers of water, strong and full of life. We will
become the vessels chosen to bring glory

to your name.

Amen!

TRAPS

Father God, we pray that you will keep us safe. Dont allow us to be tricked. Open our eyes to see the traps and snares the devil has set up to destroy us. We ask for your wisdom and guidance. Shield us with your love and we shall be protected. Dont allow us to be gullible, believing the lies of those around us. Make us wise as serpents and harmless as doves. Give us a spirit of discernment, we pray.

Amen!

TRAILBLAZERS

Father God, thank you for making us trailblazers
We will not learn the way of the heathen. We will
walk in obedience. Rebellion has no place in our
hearts. We are the head and not the tail. We are
above and not beneath. You are our shelter from
the storm, and our protection from harm.

Guide us today.

Amen!

SELF-SUFFICIENT

Father God, we believe you have accepted us as your own, so take control of our lives. Do with us, as it pleases you. Speak to us that we might know your heart. Teach us to obey your voice. Dont allow us to think that we are self-sufficient. Without you, we can do nothing. Our trust is in you. Thank you for sustaining us.

Amen!

ALL SUFFICIENCY

Father God, you are an all-sufficient God.
You are all powerful, all knowing, and you are
everywhere at the same time. Before you formed
us in our mothers wombs, you knew us and
called us to your purpose. We will go where
you send us and do what you command. We
surrender our spirit, soul and body to you.

Use us.

Amen!

DEDICATION

Father God, we dedicate every part of our bodies
to you and to the purpose you have designed for
them. We will not misuse or abuse our bodies.
We give ourselves to you. We are completely at
your disposal. Let your Word come alive in our
hearts. Anoint us with power and authority. You
are our Head. Thank you for being with us,
and delivering us in every situation.
Amen!

CONSEQUENCES

Father God, we commit to guarding our ways and actions. We know the consequences of our actions. We will remember our teachings, for they are health and life to us. Remove the desire to sin from our hearts. Hear our prayers and maintain our cause. Perfect the things, which concern us, we pray.

Amen!

SET APART

Father God, you have called us and set us apart from the world. We are in the world, but are not governed by the worlds system. You have made us a light in a world of darkness. Thank you for the strength to obey your Word. You have anointed us to do a work in the earth. You have called us to pull down, to destroy, to plant, and to build.

Amen!

TRUTH

Father God, strengthen us to stand for the truth. Give us a hunger and a thirst for what is right. Let us speak the truth in love. Let our lives be a testimony of our faith in you. Let our lives honor your holy name. Let the spirit of wisdom lead us. Keep us in the center of your will.

Amen!

VISION

Father God, we will run with the vision and fulfill our purpose. Our ears are keen to your voice. Our hearts are sensitive to your commands. You have given us hinds feet to walk upon our high places. We will not look to the left or the right, but we will keep our eyes steadfast on you.

Amen!

SERVANTS

Father God, we want you to use us. Use us to be hope for the hopeless. Use us to boldly talk about you to others. Use us to accomplish the task that is before us this day. Our victory is in you. Show yourself mighty on our behalf.

Amen!

CALMNESS

Father God, we thank you for your protection.
No evil planned against us shall prosper. All evil
intentions devised against us are destroyed by
the power of your Word. We are victorious in
you. Keep us calm and in peace. Dont allow us
to fret, but keep us focused.

Amen!

FAITHFULNESS

Father God, you are a God who cannot lie.
Whatsoever you have promised us, you will
do. You promised to always be with us in the
good times and the difficult times. We rest on
that promise. We will not depend on our own
understanding. Our hope of success is in you.
You have never failed us.
Thank you for your faithfulness today.
Amen!

MERCY

Father God, remember us in the magnitude of your mercy. You are a faithful, just, and loving God. You have covered and protected us so many times, and we need you today. We will do all that we can do, but we trust you for victory. Bring us through the seen and the unseen dangers, we pray. Thank you.

Amen!

UNETHICAL ATTACKS

Father God, we have been greatly blessed by
your presence. You have kept us safe by your
spirit. Thank you for taking care of us. You have
covered and shielded us from unethical attacks.
Thank you for your divine protection. Be with us
today as we conquer the tasks before us.

Amen!

New Day

Father God, you allowed the sun to rise and shine upon us this morning. You watched over us all through the night. Every day you protect us from hurt, harm, and danger. Thank you for this new day, which you allowed us to see. Strengthen us to take full advantage of this day. Let everything we do, bring glory to your name.

Amen!

COVERING

Father God, thank you for covering us with
your compassion and loving-kindness. Thank
you for covering us with wisdom and strength.
And, we thank you for covering us with your
love. You have enlarged our territories and given
us opportunities beyond our imagination. You
delivered us so many times, from those who lifted
up their hands against us.
Thank you for our victories.
Amen!

EXECUTION

Father God, wherever we have gone you have directed our footsteps. You have blessed our going out and our coming in. We live because of you. Our skills and talents come from you.

When we obey your voice and execute the instructions from our leaders, you make our way prosperous. Thank you for our health, healing, and deliverance.

Be with us today, we pray.

Amen!

LAWLESSNESS

Father God, we thank you for keeping us free from abuse, addiction, and violence. We thank you, that the spirit of suicide does not hover over us. We are not robbers, murderers or rapists. You have covered us, and your strength sustains us. We walk in your power today, as we go to conquer.

Amen!

TRAVELS

Father God, you have begun a work in us that only you can finish. We yield ourselves to you this day. Have your way in our lives. We thank you for our provisions and safe travels. We pray that you will refresh us. Let the words of our mouths, and the meditation of our hearts, be acceptable in your sight.

Amen!

FOUNDATION

Father God, we bless you today, because you
have placed our feet on a firm foundation.
You have established us in a secure and stable
environment. We will not become arrogant or
obnoxious. We will not forget that everything we
have came from you. Wisdom and might belong
to you, yet, every day you give them to us as we
need them. We thank you.

Amen!

ANGELS

Father God, thank you for sending your angels
to deliver us. Even as they minister around your
Throne, you allow them to minister to us. We
thank you for the angels, who are assigned to
us. Thank you, that they encamp around us, to
protect us. They carry out your Word concerning
us each day. Thank you for the angels, who
watch over us, even when we dont realize it.

Amen!

APPRECIATION

Father God, you instructed us when we didnt
know what to do. You defended us from those
who lifted up their hands against us. You
have been faithful to us. We will not take your
kindness for granted. We humble ourselves at
your feet, asking you to be with us as we move
forward in this task. We thank you for victory
through your Word.

Amen!

VICTORIES

Father God, you have loved us with an
everlasting love. You have been with us, time
after time. You fought battles and won victories
for us. You conquered battles that were too
great for us. You solved problems, which would
have defeated us. And you clarified situations,
designed to distract us. You never left us alone.
Thank you for being the victory in our lives.

Amen!

GOD

Father God, you are sovereign and excellent in power. You can do whatever you desire. You live in truth, in judgment, and in righteousness. You are God, our Master Jehovah! You have not left us destitute. You have covered us with your mercy and truth. We trust you to continue covering us.

Amen!

TRUST

Father God, thank you for access into your presence. When things are challenging we will remember your faithfulness. We will trust you, even when things look contrary. Thank you for removing the hindrances and stumbling blocks out of our way. We are blessed, because we dwell in you. Be with us today.

Amen!

SEARCH

Father God, we want you to search us and know
our hearts. Try us and know our thoughts. You
see our right and wrong doings. Cleanse us from
any wicked ways that are in us. We want your
blessings to abide with us. Bless our bread and
our water. Your mercy towards us is great. You
have removed our transgressions from us, and we
thank you.

Amen!

Appointed Time

Father God, you have reserved an appointed time
for each of us to receive our harvest. We dont
have to be jealous or envious of one another. We
will rejoice and celebrate each other. Cause us to
remember that it is you, who raise one up and put
one down. It is by your discretion, and we trust
your judgment. We will guard our hearts from
thinking evil.

Amen!

TRIUMPH

Father God, we thank you because we triumph in every situation. It is not based on wins or losses. You have anointed us to walk in victory. We thank you for the creative power you have given us. Because our hope is in you, stress and worry are destroyed from our lives. We are walking upon our high places. Thank you for every victory you have given us.

Amen!

RESIST

Father God, we will close our mouths and resist
speaking negatively. We will not speak against the
things you have promised us. Our mouths will not
speak both blessings and curses. We will not look
to the left or to the right, but we will keep our
eyes upon you. We will rest on your promises. Go
with us today and bring us to victory.

Amen!

CHARACTER

Father God, our leaders have taught us the right way. A firm foundation has been established in our hearts. The character that we possess will carry us a long way if we allow it. Let us move forward and build upon this foundation with truth and integrity. As we complete this task today, let the demonstration of your love be seen. Amen!

GOD FIRST

Father God, you have blessed us beyond measure. We will honor you by putting you first in our lives and in our finances. We will give you our best. We thank you for supplying all that we need and giving us the desires of our hearts. Thank you for all we have achieved through trusting you.

Amen!

ITS SUPERNATURAL

Father God, we believe everything we have accomplished has been supernatural; the wins, the losses, and the victories. Of ourselves we can do nothing. We believe because of you, all that belongs to us will come to us! We are appointed and anointed to accomplish our task. We desire to fulfill our calling in you. We thank you now.

Amen!

Enlarge Our Territory

Father God, you know all there is to know about us. Yet, you keep us on your mind. You accept the responsibility for us, and you seek to magnify us. All we need to do is obey you and follow your instructions. We will always come out on top, when we obey your voice.

Keep us in your will, we pray.

Amen!

PURSUE

Father God, cause us to stay focused and keep our dreams before us. You have given us the strength and power, to pursue, overtake, and conquer what is before us. Let us keep our eyes on you. We will not give up. Thank you for the hope we have in you.

We will reach the destiny you have called us to.

Amen!

FAITH

Father God, you are gracious and full of
compassion. You have made us a shining light to
all who witness our performance. Continue to use
us that your glory may be revealed, wherever we
go. Thank you that we walk by faith and not by
sight. You have conditioned our hearts and we
visualize victory, wherever we go. You made us
the head in so many difficult situations,
and we thank you.
Amen!

FAME

Father God, you have equipped us to handle fame in the integrity of our hearts. We recognize that who we are and hope to become are not in our talents, but in you. Thank you for leaders who taught us to work hard, but our talent is your gift to us.

Help us to safeguard and use our gift wisely.

Amen!

THE DIAMOND

Father God, help us see ourselves through your eyes. Let us see how valuable we are to you. Let your will be done in us. Help us to keep moving forward and not lose sight of the prize. We will not be distracted with the sword of the enemy. We will not walk in fear. We will complete this task in faith, seeing and doing it your way. Your truth has been our shield and buckler. We walk in the true value of who we are and whose we are.

Amen!

JOY

Father God, we come asking you to purge our hearts, so we wont yield to the sins of our flesh. Let your joy remain with us, because your joy is our strength. Despite what we go through, we are glad that you are with us. You have done more for us than we could have ever imagined. Thank you for your cleansing power.

Amen!

SPECIAL

Father God, we are the apple of your eye. We thank you for equipping us to do the things you have assigned to us. With you, all things are possible. Thank you that our hands are blessed to accomplish our assignments. Teach us to rejoice with one another. Thank you for making each of us special to you.

Amen!

REST

Father God, direct our lives according to your will and plan. We will rest upon your Word. As your eyes go back and forth in all the earth, look on us and take control of everything that concerns us. We put no confidence in our flesh. We dont know how to direct our steps, but you do. Deliver us from ourselves that we may wholly follow you.

Amen!

Every Day

Father God, let peace and truth abide with us all the days of our lives. Let humility be our strength. We will bridle our tongue and maintain our peace. We will not speak contrary to your Word. Your Word says, we can do it, and you are with us to deliver us. We choose to believe your Word. We know there is no failure in you. Our best strategy is to run to you. To achieve our goals, it is in our best interest to stay close to you.

Amen!

UNMOVABLE

Father God, in you we live, move, and have the activities of our limbs. We are more than conquerors through you, who love us. We need you to fortify our walk with you, until our hearts are fixed on you, and our steps are unmovable. Let us stand still and see your salvation. Do a work in us, which cannot be denied. Let all that see it, glorify your name.

Thank you for our deliverance.

Amen.

SAY YES

Father God, let our answer to you always be,
yes. Despite what comes against us, let us say,
The Will of the Lord be done. We believe that
you desire the best for us. You delight to show
yourself strong on our behalf. Enlarge our hearts
to love you more.
We are grateful for all the things you do for us.
Today we say, yes to you.
Amen!

TREES

Father God, you have been so good to us. Every day we remember your faithfulness. We will speak of you among the heathens and not be ashamed. We are like trees planted by rivers of water, which bring forth our fruit in our season. You have blessed the works of our hands and caused us to prosper. Thank you.

Amen!

CREATED

Father God, you have shaped and fashioned us with your own hands. We thank you that we are fearfully and wonderfully made, and marvelous are your works. Thank you for goodness and mercy, which follow us all the days of our lives. You are our strength and you will make our feet like hinds' feet. We will walk upon our high places and conquer. Victory is ours today. Amen!

THE BEST

Father God, we dont always understand your ways, but we know whatever you allow is whats best for us. When we lose and feel defeated, you are the lifter of our heads. When we are disappointed, you shield us and keep us from developing bad attitudes. You have surrounded us and we will not lose heart. When others dug pits for us, they fell into the ditches, which they made. Their mischief shall return upon their own heads; and their violence shall dwell in the midst of them. We thank you for all things.

Amen!

BOOKS
WRITTEN
BY
RENA BOSTON

THE PROVERBS 31 MAN and HIS WOMAN

This book unveils the Proverbs 31 Man and the heart of his Woman. She will do him good and not evil. She is his companion and not his slave. She is his partner and not his competitor. They recognize and appreciate each others value. The content is based on the truths contained in The Book of Proverbs, which is a Manual for Life. There is no dowry that can contain what the Word of God teaches, or where the Holy Spirit leads. This book is for everyone; single and married, men and women! It addresses the challenges and victories of life. Start reading today!   *(10/01/16)*

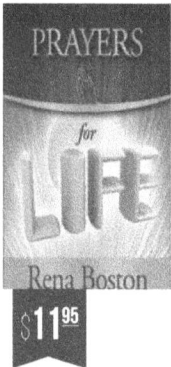

$10⁰⁰

PRAYERS for LIFE

This book was written to promote prayer in our daily lives. It contains fully scripted Bible-based, faith-filled prayers. The theme is: Prayer is to our spirit, what breath is to the body; LIFE!   *(4/12/16)*

$11⁹⁵

NO SCARS

Raven was on the verge of insanity; yet, she escaped with No Scars. The evidence of her sufferings was wiped away. It was so dramatic that it was almost unbelievable. Slowly stepping forward, Raven contemplated her image in the mirror. The reflection she saw and its persona overwhelmed her. She did not look like what she had gone through! She didnt even look like her original image; she was better!   *(1/20/15)*

$11⁹⁵

MONEY, the MASTER or the SERVANT

This book is a must-read! However, you may find yourself laughing and crying at the same time. It may even feel like a roller coaster ride, but I assure you theres a safe landing. It is designed to motivate you to become the Master of your Money and sharpen your awareness of moneys proper place as a Servant. Learn how to allow your money to serve you. As you stroll with me on this debt- free journey, you will experience a freedom and a thirst to assume control of your money immediately. *(10/29/14)*

HOPES, DREAMS, VISIONS

This motivational handbook revitalizes the heart, stimulates the mind, and provides strength to conquer obstacles in life. It contains 60 scenarios designed to elevate the readers expectations of themselves. It is also designed to boost their willpower and commitment against any resistance and limitations. *(August 2013)*

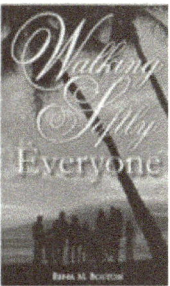

WALKING SOFTLY for EVERYONE

This book contains a special message for everyone. It encourages the discouraged, cautions the singles, massages the heart of the divorced, and prepares the married for a life of challenge and love. *(April 2007)*

WALKING SOFTLY CALENDAR

This calendar contains 12 poems surrounding love-walking.
The power to feel love, find love, and experience love are on every page.
The monthly challenges are designed to create an atmosphere
of sensitivity and warmth.   *(October 2005)*

$12⁹⁵

IF ONLY Motivational CD

Have you ever made excuses you knew were unacceptable?
After all, self-preservation is all about excuses; our reasons and
justifications for doing and saying; what we do and say.
Stop allowing excuses to stunt your growth!   *(June 2005)*

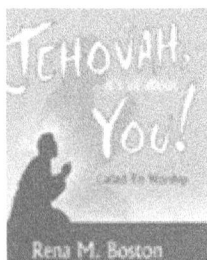

$7⁰⁰

JEHOVAH, ITS ALL ABOUT YOU-CD

This CD contains the Jehovah worship book PLUS several
worship songs intermittently sung by Renown Artist, Kenneth
L. Daniel Sr. Allow this CD to move you into a powerful worship
experience with God.   *(June 2005)*

$15⁰⁰

JEHOVAH, ITS ALL ABOUT YOU-BOOK

Have you ever been Center-Stage with God? Use this book during your devotions and it will move you into a powerful worship experience with God. *(September 2004)*

$7⁹⁵

WALKING SOFTLY II

Part Two of the Walking Softly Book Collection reveals new ideas to invigorate your relationship. It is for anyone who is in love, waiting for love, and those who are not sure about love. *(August 2004)*

$12⁹⁵

WALKING SOFTLY I

A book of poetry designed to help keep love alive. It creates an intimate ambiance to discuss ugly issues and helps men and women express their feelings. It brings warmth to ice cold settings. This book is a must read *(June 2003)*

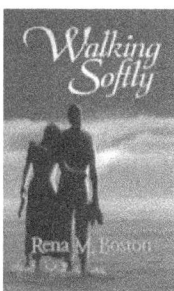

$12⁹⁵

OTHER AUTHORS BOOKS
PUBLISHED BY JUST WRITERS

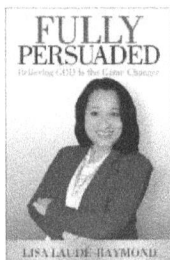

$14⁹⁹

FULLY PERSUADED
Believing GOD is the Game Changer

In Fully Persuaded, Lisa shares her story of how embracing her faith empowered her to take «professional leaps,» and laid the foundation for her professional success. Read:
 how Lisa succeeded in checking off the top item on her bucket list,
 how she clinched her dream job, overseas,
 how she secured a career dominated by the wealthy, while she was
  seemingly broke,
 how GOD sent her career to find her, instead of her finding it,
 how she moved from being a professional coach to her girlfriends to
  becoming an executive coach to CEOs, and more...

(March 2017)

$19⁹⁵

HUMILITY Before HONOUR

This hardcover book is a must read. It is a keepsake for generations to come. Bishop Carlis Lee Moody, Sr.s biography will reveal a man of faith and integrity . He has travelled the globe fulfilling the great commission in over 42 countries. He is an international symbol
of hope to those he serves.
(October 2005)

Just Writers Publishing Company
"Where Fingers Write From the Heart"

www.ingramcontent.com/pod-product-compliance
Lightning Source LLC
Chambersburg PA
CBHW021930040426
42448CB00008B/998